MY FAMILY REMEMBERS
The 1950s

Kath Walker

FRANKLIN WATTS
LONDON • SYDNEY

First published in 2011 by
Franklin Watts
338 Euston Road, London NW1 3BH

Franklin Watts Australia
Level 17/207 Kent Street, Sydney NSW 2000

© 2011 Franklin Watts

ISBN: 978 1 4451 0102 6

Dewey classification number: 941'.0855

A CIP catalogue record for this publication is available from the British Library.

Printed in China

Franklin Watts is a division of Hachette Children's Books, an Hachette UK Company.

www.hachette.co.uk

Planned and produced by Discovery Books Ltd., 2 College Street,
Ludlow, Shropshire, SY8 1AN
www.discoverybooks.net
Editor: James Nixon
Design: Blink Media

Photo credits: Corbis: pp. 16 bottom (BBC), 17 top (Sunset Boulevard); Getty Images: pp. 6 bottom-right (Thurston Hopkins/Stringer), 7 middle (Terry Fincher/Stringer), 12 top (SSPL), 19 right (Chris Ware/Stringer), 21 top (Popperfoto), 25 top (SSPL), 28 right (SSPL), 29 top (Hulton Archive); Mary Evans Picture Library: pp. 13 middle (Interfoto Agentur), 14 top (Classic Stock/H Armstrong Roberts), 23 bottom-left (Henry Grant); Peter and John Nixon: pp. 20 top-right, 20 bottom, 26 top, 28 left; Shutterstock: p. 18 top (Patricia Hofmeester); Wikimedia: pp. 7 bottom, 12 right, 14 bottom, 15 bottom (Gregory F Maxwell), 18 bottom (Metro-Goldwyn-Mayer), 19 left, 26 bottom-left (Charles01), bottom-right (Malcolma), 27 bottom (Brian Forbes); www.picturethepast.org: pp. 8 top and left (Courtesy of Nottingham City Council), 9 top (Courtesy of Derby City Council), 10 top (Courtesy of Newark Advertiser), 11 top (Courtesy of Edgar Lloyd), 13 top (Courtesy of Buxton Museum & Art Gallery), 22 top (Courtesy of W E Middleton & Son), 23 top (Courtesy of Derbyshire Local Studies Libraries), 24 bottom (Courtesy of Wood Collection), 25 bottom (Courtesy of Nottingham City Council), 27 top (Courtesy of G H F Atkins).

Cover photos: Mary Evans Picture Library: right (Interfoto Agentur).

Every attempt has been made to clear copyright. Should there be any inadvertent omission please apply to the publisher for rectification.

Words that are **bold** in the text are explained in the glossary.

Note to parents and teachers
Every effort has been made by the Publishers to ensure that the websites in this book are suitable for children, that they are of the highest educational value, and that they contain no inappropriate or offensive material. However, because of the nature of the Internet, it is impossible to guarantee that the contents of these sites will not be altered. We strongly advise that Internet access is supervised by a responsible adult.

Contents

 Downloadable activity and information sheets are available at www.franklinwatts.co.uk

Meet the families

This book looks at life in the 1950s. World War II had ended in 1945, but hard times continued into the early '50s. However, as the decade progressed life became easier in many ways with new and exciting changes. Four children's parents and grandparents share their memories of those days.

Alice

Tony

Stan

June

Alice's family

Alice Hibberd is 13 years old. She has an older sister called Meg and lives with her mother, Julie, and stepfather, Tony. Tony was a young child in the '50s. Close by live Alice's grandparents, Stan and June, who were born in the 1930s and were in their twenties during the '50s.

Sarah

Sarah's family

Sarah Hadland is 12 years old and lives with her older brother, Jacob, and parents, Marcia and Dan. Her grandmother, Ruby, was born in Jamaica in the 1930s and moved to the UK in the 1950s when she was in her twenties.

Ruby

Matty

Hazel

Matty's family

Matty Morris was born in 1998 and lives with his parents, Julie and Kevin. He has a younger sister called Milly and an older brother called Peter. His grandparents, Derek and Linda, were born in the 1940s. They were young children in the '50s. Derek was aged between 6 and 15 while Linda was aged between 3 and 12.

Hazel's family

Hazel Stancliffe was born in the year 2000. She lives with her older sister, Lily, and her parents, Abigail and Paul. Her grandmother, Jean, and step-grandfather, Adrian, were born in the 1940s and they became teenagers in the 1950s.

Derek

Linda

Adrian

Jean

After the war

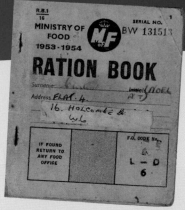

Britain in the 1950s was still recovering from the effects of World War II (1939–1945). Many buildings had been destroyed by bombs. Some goods were in short supply and items such as soap, meat, sugar and eggs were rationed. **Rationing** did not completely end until 1954.

Alice asks her grandmother about rationing:

We were allowed just 2 ounces (57 grammes) of butter each – and it had to last a whole week! We'd take our ration books into town when we went shopping. After we handed over our coupons, the shopkeeper would cut the piece of butter off a big block and carefully wrap it up in paper.

Reminders of the war were everywhere. These were air raid shelters, **bomb sites** and concrete defences. Men in army uniform were still a common sight. All men aged between 17 and 21 had to spend two years in the **armed forces.**

This gun tower was one of many buildings left standing long after World War II had ended.

Empty bomb sites were now places where children played games.

6

Hazel asks her step-grandfather about food shortages:
There was a worry that children were getting unhealthy because of the food shortages. So the government supplied us with free orange juice. I remember going with my mother to the village hall to collect it. We were also given free cod liver oil, which I had a spoonful of every day. Most of my friends thought it tasted horrible, but I didn't mind it.

'We were given free cod liver oil.'

Children mob a sweetshop on the day sweet rationing ended.

To lift people's spirits, the government launched the Festival of Britain in 1951. This was an exhibition in London celebrating British achievements in **industry**, science and the arts. A funfair at the exhibition created a party atmosphere.

Visitors at the Festival of Britain stop for a rest outside the 'Dome of Discovery' science exhibition.

Places to live

In the early 1950s, there were not enough houses. Wartime bombs had destroyed about two million homes.

In 1955, half of all British houses were more than 65 years old and many needed modernising. Some of the older ones did not even have indoor toilets. New homes of the '50s had bathrooms and hot and cold running water.

During the '50s, many homes like these were torn down. How would you like having to use these outdoor toilets (left)?

Alice asks her grandmother what her house was like:

In the early 1950s, I lived with my parents in a house that had been built before the war. We didn't have hot water from a tap. If we wanted a wash or bath we had to boil the water first on the cooker or fire.

'We didn't have hot water from a tap.'

Sarah asks her grandmother about where she lived:
I lived in a big old semi-detached house that I shared with several other single people. We had some hot water in the bathroom to wash with, but not a lot. To have a proper bath, I would pay to go to the public baths once a week.

Through the decade, old and damaged buildings were torn down and replaced with new housing estates.

To stop cities becoming crowded whole new towns were built. Where there was not much space, homes were built as flats in high tower blocks.

New houses like these were built by councils throughout Britain during the 1950s.

Alice asks her stepfather about his house:
I was born in 1948 and shortly afterwards my parents were given a house by the **local council**. Ours was a corner house and the last to be built on the estate. This was really lucky because we had the 'luxury' of two toilets – one in the bathroom and one downstairs.

Alice's stepfather took this photo of his friends playing on the estate where he lived.

Going shopping

Shopping for food in the 1950s usually meant visiting several small shops, such as the butcher's, baker's and **greengrocer's**. Most people did not have a fridge to keep food fresh, so they shopped for items such as meat and fish every day. Milk, bread and groceries were often delivered to the door.

Instead of supermarkets, people bought their food from small shops that sold just one or two types of food.

Hazel asks her step-grandfather about shopping:
We didn't have a fridge until 1956, so we used the cold stone floor of the larder to keep milk fresh. Unlike today, all shops closed at 5.00 or 5.30 pm and nothing opened on Sundays.

'We didn't have a fridge until 1956.'

The money shoppers used was different from today. It was in pounds (£), shillings (s) and pence (d), with 12 pennies to a shilling and 20 shillings to a pound. Imagine what it was like to add up £1 11s 6d and £5 15s 10d! The answer to the sum is £7 7s 4d.

Here is a ten shilling note and the coins that people paid with in the '50s. The largest coin was called a 'half crown' and was worth 2s 6d (12.5p).

TIME DIFFERENCE

Shopping basket:

1950

1 dozen eggs – 9p (1s 10d)
pint of milk – 2p (5d)
loaf of bread – 2.5p (6d)

Now

1 dozen eggs – £2.40
pint of milk – 45p
loaf of bread – £1.10

A girl chooses a toy from a stall at the market.

Many people would buy food from local shops but make a trip into town for other goods such as clothes or to visit a weekly market. Going to town was a chance to stop and chat with friends.

Here is Alice's grandmother, June (left), on a shopping trip with a friend.

Alice asks her stepfather what the shops were like:

When we went shopping in town, there was a large shop called Baileys that amazed me. A sales assistant would put your money into a small metal container above his or her head and then send it flying on wires across the shop to the pay desk. The cashier would take the money out, put a receipt and any change inside the container and send it whizzing back towards us.

Life at home

In 1951, less than one-quarter of married women went out to work. Most wives were busy doing the housework. Many homes did not have washing machines, so laundry was done by hand. Housewives also spent a lot of time preparing meals.

Some housewives used a **mangle** on washdays to squeeze the water out of wet laundry.

Alice asks her stepfather about washdays:
Monday was washday and the whole house smelled of laundry. Mum did the washing by hand, by rubbing the clothes hard against a ridged **washboard**. Then she would squeeze the water out using the mangle we kept in the shed. If things like sheets needed to be boiled, we used a 'copper'. This was a large copper container which we filled with buckets of cold water. It had gas burners underneath that heated the water up.

Washboard

Sarah asks her grandmother how she did her laundry:
There was no washing machine in the house I shared. We used to wash our clothes by hand and then take turns to dry them by the fire.

'We used to wash our clothes by hand.'

However, housework was getting easier. People could afford more labour-saving devices, such as vacuum cleaners and electric cookers. There were new, easy-to-clean materials for the home, such as stainless steel and plastic.

What electrical goods for the home can you see in this 1950s shop window?

People were also spending more money on patterned wallpaper and colourful fabrics to brighten their homes. A growing number of households had telephones, **record players** and televisions, but very few had central heating.

Record players built into cabinets were popular in the '50s.

Hazel asks her step-grandfather how his home was heated:
We lived in a small bungalow. It was freezing cold in the winter. The coal fire was in the living room and father would get up early every morning to lay and light it. There was no heat in the bedrooms, so we kept ourselves warm with hot water bottles and lots of blankets.

Having fun

Children in the 1950s spent a lot more time playing outdoors than they do today. There was much less television to watch and no home computers. Less traffic meant that streets were safer places for playing games like football, cricket or hopscotch and to master the latest craze – hula hoops.

The craze for hula hoops started in the late '50s. You had to keep a plastic hoop spinning around your waist.

Alice asks her stepfather where he played:

Outside our house we had grass areas each side of the road with silver birch trees that we used as cricket stumps. The roads were made up of concrete slabs with lines of black tar between them that made brilliant tennis courts. There wasn't much traffic around then, so our game didn't get stopped very often. I always felt very safe going out to play.

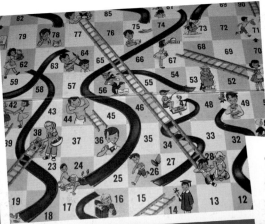

Board games such as snakes and ladders, ludo and draughts were popular at the time.

Alice's stepfather, Tony, and his brother play on their bikes.

This snakes and ladders board from the 1950s has slides instead of snakes.

Favourite boys' toys included train sets, Meccano sets, and model aeroplane kits. For the girls, there were dolls, along with prams and cots to put them in.

The train set was a favourite children's toy in the '50s.

A boy settles down with his dad to read his weekly comic.

Many children looked forward to a weekly comic, and there were plenty to choose from. There was *The Beano*, *The Dandy* and *The Topper*. Older girls often bought the comic *Girl*, which had craft activities and articles about famous people.

'We loved listening to the radio.'

Hazel asks her step-grandfather about radio shows:

We loved listening to the radio. The science fiction **serial** *Journey Into Space* was a great favourite – except with my little brother who would hide in the kitchen when it came on! We always had our Sunday lunch with the radio on.

Here is a radio from the 1950s.

Television and film

At the start of the 1950s, only a small number of homes had television sets. Then in June 1953, many people bought or hired sets to watch the **coronation** of Queen Elizabeth II.

People up and down the country had parties to celebrate the Queen's coronation.

Matty asks his grandmother about her first television:
My parents bought our first black-and-white TV set so we could watch the Queen's coronation in 1953. We were very excited about the whole thing. My grandparents and the neighbours came over to watch it with us – it felt like a big party.

'My parents bought our first black-and-white TV set in 1953.'

Television was in black and white in the '50s and the BBC was the only channel until 1955, when ITV started. At that time there were about eight hours of television a day. Children enjoyed programmes such as *Blue Peter* and *The Adventures of Robin Hood*.

Andy Pandy was a popular children's TV show about a puppet who lived in a picnic basket.

Ben Hur was a hit film of 1959 set in ancient Rome.

As television became more popular, people went to the cinema less. However many still made weekly trips to the 'pictures' and there were Saturday morning cinema clubs for children. Across the country, the clubs showed a mixture of stories, cartoons and comedies.

Hazel asks her step-grandfather what he watched on television:

We didn't get a TV until 1955. Before that I used to go to the next door neighbour's house every Friday evening at 5.00 pm to see cowboy programmes, such as *The Cisco Kid* or *Hopalong Cassidy*.

Cowboy films and TV shows made lots of children want to play at being cowboys.

Sounds of the '50s

Many homes in the 1950s had record players that played music on large black discs. At the start of the decade, there was no pop music for young people. But then new types of music came along that changed everything.

Hazel asks her step-grandfather what music he listened to:

We listened to our parents' records by singers such as Bing Crosby. I remember walking down the street in light rain with my younger brother singing *Just Walkin' in the Rain*, a big hit from American singer Johnny Ray in 1956.

There was skiffle, a type of **folk music** with lots of rhythm. It was played by small groups who used household objects such as washboards as instruments. Then came rock 'n' roll. This loud, energetic music from the USA became popular in Britain in the mid-'50s. *Rock Around the Clock* by Bill Haley & His Comets and *All Shook Up* by Elvis Presley were big hits.

Singer Elvis Presley who became known as 'the King of Rock and Roll'.

Bill Haley & His Comets singing *Rock Around the Clock*, a huge hit of 1955.

In the '50s, most towns had at least one dance hall where live music played. If the music was rock 'n' roll, young couples twirled around dancing the 'jive'.

'My brother would play the drums on saucepans!'

Alice asks her stepfather what music he liked:

We got our first radiogram in the '50s. It was a piece of furniture that combined a radio and a record player. I loved Lonnie Donegan, who played skiffle music. My brother and I used to muck about trying to make our own skiffle music. He would play the drums on saucepans!

Fashions

At the start of the '50s, young children's clothes were not casual and colourful like they are today. The girls wore dresses often with cardigans, while boys wore short trousers. Grown-up men wore suits and hats for a lot of the time while women mostly wore dresses or skirts and blouses.

These boys are wearing dungarees with their smart shirts and ties.

Young girls in the '50s often wore bows in their hair and sandals on their feet.

The young teenage boy in this photo is wearing his first grown-up suit.

Alice asks her stepfather how people dressed:
I remember clothes being quite drab, all greys and browns. There was hardly any colour around. Mum had a simple shapeless coat and dad would never go into town without a jacket and tie.

Before the 1950s, the word 'teenager' was not used. Around the age of 14, young people would stop dressing as children and start wearing the same type of clothes as their parents. But this changed as young people developed their own style of dressing.

Teenage girls began wearing circular skirts, often with several stiff **petticoats** underneath. Hair was worn short, in a ponytail or backcombed into a high 'beehive' style. Some boys wore jeans and a leather jacket and combed their hair back into a **quiff**. There was also a group of teenagers called **Teddy boys**, who stood out with their narrow trousers, long jackets with velvet collars, thin ties and thick-soled shoes.

Hazel asks her step-grandfather what clothes he wore:

We wore school uniform most of the time. For me this was a grey shirt and grey shorts. We didn't have lots of different clothes like children do today. My dad wore a suit and hat nearly all the time. Here is a photo of him wearing a suit on the beach when we were on holiday!

'My dad wore a suit and hat nearly all the time.'

Schooldays

In the 1950s, many new schools had to be built to replace old or war-damaged buildings. The new schools were built in a fresh, modern style.

The new schools of the '50s were lighter and brighter than older schools.

All children had to go to school between the ages of 5 and 15. At age 11, children at primary school sat an exam called the 11 Plus. Those who passed it usually went on to **grammar school** where they could study until age 18. Those who failed went to a **secondary modern school** for four more years.

Hazel asks her step-grandfather about his school uniform:

Here is a picture of me (far right) in my uniform. We wore grey suits in the winter and blazers with **flannels** in the summer. The schools were very strict about uniform, especially the school cap, which most of us hated. In my final year in 1959, I didn't have to wear a cap anymore. I was so happy and celebrated by throwing it in the dustbin.

Blackboards, wall maps and a radio are the only pieces of equipment in this 1950s classroom.

Instead of the whiteboards that schools have today, classrooms had blackboards that the teacher wrote on in chalk. Classes would often have to copy work from the blackboard or textbook in silence. Pupils behaving badly might get a beating with a cane or slipper.

Matty asks his grandmother about her schooldays:

School life was very strict. I remember the bigger boys playing conkers in the playground. Once one of them got his conker stuck on an overhead cable and threw an empty milk bottle at it to get it down. The bottle smashed and cut my leg. The boy was given the cane in front of me for what he had done. I felt very sorry for him.

We wrote with pens that had to be dipped in ink. Blobs of ink used to spill all over our paper and make a terrible mess. The ink was kept in inkwells in our desk.

'Blobs of ink used to spill all over our paper.'

Inkwell

Cane

At work

In '50s Britain there were plenty of jobs for people. There were lots of factories making items such as cars and electrical goods. Compared to today thousands more people were employed in industries such as mining and shipbuilding.

A team of steelworkers take a break in 1955. The '50s was a good time for the steel industry.

A coal miner hard at work in the 1950s.

Wages were quickly rising. But working women were not getting a fair deal. They were only paid about half as much as men for doing the same work.

TIME DIFFERENCE

In 1950, the average weekly wage was £7 5s 9d (£7.29) and by 1957 it had risen to £12. Today's average wage is about £531 per week.

There was actually a shortage of workers in the '50s. Thousands of people from Caribbean islands, such as Jamaica, came to Britain to work. Many of these **immigrants** got jobs working on trains or buses, or in hospitals. Some were treated badly because of their race.

Sarah asks her grandmother how she found work:

I came to England from Jamaica in the middle of the 1950s with my sister. We were told there was plenty of work and we planned to return home when we had made a bit of money... but we're still here! The **racism** made life very hard at times. Sometimes we would turn up for a job but there would be a sign in the window saying 'Vacancies – no coloureds'.

Immigrants from the Caribbean arrive in Britain in 1955.

'We planned to return home when we had made a bit of money.'

Alice asks her grandfather about the work he did:

I worked on a farm in the '50s. Things were changing as new farm machinery came into use. In 1955 we got our first milking machine, which sped things up a lot. Before that, we milked the cows by hand. It took an hour to milk eight or nine cows.

Tractors became cheaper in the '50s and so more farmers could afford to have one.

Getting about

The family in this photo are enjoying a day out in their car.

As petrol rationing ended and wages rose, more people were buying cars or motorbikes. This gave people greater freedom to come and go and made travelling long distances easier.

More lorries were also being used for transporting goods around the country. The roads got a lot busier. In 1959 Britain's first motorway – the M1 – opened between London and Leeds. There was no speed limit on it then.

Hazel asks her step-grandfather about '50s cars:

We didn't have a car, but our neighbour was always happy to give us a lift if we needed one. Some cars had little yellow arms that popped out of the side of the car to show which direction you were turning. Sometimes they jammed and you had to bang the inside of the car to make them go up or down!

A 1950s Morris Oxford.

VFO 847

Sarah asks her grandmother how she travelled:
We used to get thick fogs in Birmingham called **smogs** that were caused by pollution. They were so thick that you couldn't see a thing and had no idea where you were. I caught the bus into work and a man holding a lantern would have to walk in front of us to guide the bus through the smog. It took ages.

Because there were a lot fewer car owners in the '50s than today, more people travelled on buses, coaches and trains. Trolley buses were powered by overhead, electricity cables.

The poles at the top of this trolley bus draw electricity from overhead cables.

TIME DIFFERENCE

In 1955, 27 per cent of distance travelled was by car or van, 17 per cent was by rail and 42 per cent was by bus and coach. Now 84 per cent of distance travelled is by car or van, 7 per cent is by rail and just 6 per cent is by bus or coach.

In the early 1950s all trains were steam-powered and poured out smoke as they chugged and puffed across the country.

Gleneagles

Holiday time

In the 1950s, more workers were getting holiday time with pay, so more families could afford to take trips away from home. Most families spent their holidays in Britain. They often stayed in **guesthouses** or hotels at seaside resorts and enjoyed the fun of the pier.

A family enjoys a ride at a seaside funfair in Blackpool, 1953.

CONEY BEACH
PORTHCAWL

WATER CHUTE

OUTINGS
to Britain's Brightest Pleasure Beach
WRITE MANAGER, CONEY BEACH, PORTHCAWL FOR ILLUSTRATED BOOKLETS AND MENUS   BRITISH RAILWAYS

Beaches like this one were very popular with holidaymakers and day trippers.

Matty asks his grandfather where he went on holiday:

Our holidays were spent in rented cottages by the sea in Wales. My mother would drive us down there by car but dad was always busy at work and could only join us for a day or two. We would go on walks, collect shells and if we were lucky we got ice cream as a special treat.

Holiday camps, such as Butlin's, provided accommodation in wooden huts, meals and lots of organised entertainment. Cheerful staff in bright uniforms encouraged everyone to take part in the activities. There were games, dancing, fun rides and competitions to find the most glamorous grannies and the knobbliest knees.

TIME DIFFERENCE

By the end of the '50s, two million British people were taking holidays abroad. Today, the British are taking about 39 million holidays abroad.

A beauty contest at a Butlin's holiday camp in 1952. The girls are wearing masks so they are judged on their figures!

Alice asks her stepfather what sort of holidays he had:

When I was seven we went to Butlin's in Minehead and stayed in a row of huts. We were woken up at 7.00 am every morning to the loud sound of *Zippidy Doo Dah*…. You couldn't escape this, as loudspeakers were built into every room. I preferred our holidays in Cornwall where we stayed in a caravan [right]. Here is a picture of some of the friends I made on holiday.

Find out what your family remembers

Try asking members of your family what they remember about the 1950s. You could ask them the same questions that children in this book have asked and then compare the answers you get. Ask your relatives how they think that life in the '50s was different from today. Get them to talk about their favourite memories or important events of the time. This will help you build up your own picture of life in the 1950s. It will also help you find out more about your family history.

This Russian postage stamp shows the satellite *Sputnik 1* orbiting the Earth.

Timeline

1951 Festival of Britain.

1952 The Great Smog, a thick fog caused by pollution, affects London. Thousands die from illness as a result.
The first Teddy Boys appear in London.
King George VI dies and his daughter Elizabeth becomes queen.

1953 Coronation of Queen Elizabeth II.
Edmund Hillary and Tenzing Norgay climb Mount Everest.

1954 Roger Bannister becomes first person to run a mile in under four minutes.
Rationing ends.

1955 Bill Haley's *Rock Around the Clock* is a major hit.

1956 Suez Crisis between Britain and Egypt leads to return of fuel rationing.
Elvis Presley's *Heartbreak Hotel* reaches no. 2 in the UK charts.

1957 *Sputnik 1*, launched into space by the Russians, is the first satellite to orbit the Earth.

1958 The first American satellite *Explorer I* is launched into space.
Munich air disaster: a plane carrying the Manchester United Football team crashes killing 20 people on board, including 8 players.

1959 First section of the M1 motorway opens.

Glossary

armed forces
The country's military forces, including the army, navy and air force.

bomb site
An area where buildings have been destroyed by bombs.

coronation
The ceremony where a king or queen is crowned.

flannels
Trousers or blazers made of soft woven wool.

folk music
A type of pop music based on older, traditional songs and tunes.

grammar school
A secondary school where children who passed their 11 Plus exam could go. Pupils studied for exams and could prepare for going to college or university.

greengrocer
A shopkeeper who sells fruit and vegetables.

guesthouse
A private home that offers accommodation to paying guests.

industry
A business or the work of making goods to sell.

immigrant
Someone who moves to another country, usually to live there permanently.

local council
A group of people responsible for the day-to-day running of a village, town or larger area.

mangle
A machine with rollers turned by a handle. Wet laundry is put between the rollers to squeeze out the water.

petticoat
A piece of clothing worn by women or girls underneath a skirt or dress.

quiff
A lock of hair brushed upward from the forehead. This hairstyle was popular with Teddy Boys and teenagers in the 1950s.

racism
When people believe that some races are better than others and treat people of other races or colour badly.

rationing
When people are only allowed to buy a fixed amount of food or other goods because of shortages.

record player
A machine with a turntable for playing and listening to records or discs.

secondary modern school
A school where children who failed their 11 Plus exam would go. Pupils focused on practical subjects such as woodwork and cookery.

serial
Something produced in parts or episodes, such as a book, a television drama or a film.

smog
A fog that has become mixed with smoke or some other type of pollution. Many British cities suffered bad smogs in the 1950s and 1960s.

Teddy boy
Member of a group of young men in the 1950s and 1960s who dressed in long jackets with thin ties.

washboard
A board with a ridged surface, used for rubbing clothes against to get them clean when washing.

Further information

Books:
The 1950s (I Can Remember), by Sally Hewitt, Franklin Watts, 2003
The 1950s (Picture History of the 20th Century), by Richard Tames, Sea to Sea Publications, 2005
Toys and Fun in the 1940s and 1950s (Family Scrapbook), by Faye Gardner, Evans, 2006

Websites:
This website has photographs and information about life in the 1950s:
http://www.woodlands-junior.kent.sch.uk/Homework/war/1950s.html

Find out what television programmes were like in the 1950s on:
http://www.whirligig-tv.co.uk/

To find out about the types of food people ate in the 1950s, go to:
http://www.eatwell.gov.uk/healthydiet/seasonsandcelebrations/howweusedtoeat/1950s/

Index